F*#%
THIS

FIND YOUR BREATH

MEDITATION IS HARD FOR EVERYONE.
YOU'RE NOT SPECIAL.

JOSH KRAFT

KREATIVE STUDIOS

Kreative Studios, LLC
Lutz Florida

ISBN (Print Edition): 978-1-66789-630-4
ISBN (eBook Edition): 978-1-66789-631-1

For more information and or other Kreative Studios products
Please visit kreativestudios.org

Edited by
Rachel Small

Cover design by
Andrew Max Storch

A percentage of all Kreative Studios sales will go to further research
on depression and mental health awareness.
Thank you for your support.

This book is dedicated to my Mom and Dad.

Thank you for everything.

I love you both.

-Josher

CONTENTS

PART THREE: THE PRACTICE

AUTHOR'S NOTE

I want to tell you how getting hit by a truck made me a happier person.

"How could someone possibly be better off after a serious motorcycle accident?" A very good question. After all, it resulted in several unpleasant side effects:

- End of career

- Surgeries

- Chronic pain

- Various impairments

But wait, Josh! Don't forget the long-term neurological effects:

- Difficulty with memory

- PTSD

- Depression

- Anxiety disorder

- Difficulty with memory

Not to mention having to work with medical staff, therapists, insurance companies, and lawyers. And dealing with all the delightful paperwork they require for their services.

So after all that pain and hassle, how could I possibly say, regularly, "I'm grateful for that accident"? I came out on the other side a happier Josh in large part because of brilliant doctors and nurses, loving parents and family members, and constant support from friends, old and new. But the biggest contributing factor in my newfound happiness? Meditation.

Meditation is how I learned to become self-aware. Meditation is how I learned to live in the moment more.

I used to be a pretty pissed-off guy. After I started meditating, over time, I didn't feel as angry and frustrated. I didn't lose my temper nearly as much. I slept better and woke up not dreading the day. If you're anything like I was, "Ugh" might be your first thought upon waking. What a shit way to start the day, huh?

"What's all this then? Some Seth Rogan look-alike trying to write a self-help book?"

Well . . . yeah. Because meditation didn't just help me through a rough couple of years—it changed my entire outlook on life.

I'm going to share with you a few meditation techniques I've learned, a few I've come up with myself, and a handful of funny stories. My hope, first and foremost, is that you don't get hit by a fucking truck. And I also hope that this book helps you see that meditation is for everyone, not just monks and yoga folk. Every single person can benefit from this practice.

So find a comfy chair, tell everyone in the house to shut up, and get reading. What do you have to lose? Who knows, maybe you'll come out the other side of this book a happier you.

PART ONE:

THE BACKSTORY

WHY *FUCK THIS?*

For a book on meditation, self-awareness, and living in the moment, *Fuck This* might seem aggressive. And it is. It's powerful.

We hear people say "fuck this" all the time, whether it's

- "Fuck this job"
- "Fuck this pen"
- "Fuck this relationship"
- "Fuck this car"
- "Fuck this book"

No matter the significance (or lack thereof) of the issue, you can say "fuck this." And each time you say those magic words, what you're doing is making a choice. A conscious decision, if you will.

CHOICES, CHOICES

Conscious decisions are the result of thousands of subconscious thoughts—thoughts you're not aware of. It's believed that the human brain has over 6,000 conscious thoughts per day.[1] Let's break that down—because that's a lot of thinking.

---

1   Crystal Raypole, "How Many Thoughts Do You Have Each Day? And Other Things to Think

For those of you who didn't pull out the calculator, there are 86,400 seconds in a day. Of those 86,400 seconds, we're generally awake for 57,600. If we were to have a new thought every 6.5 seconds (a plausible number), we'd have 8,861+ trains of thought per day. By "train of thought," I'm referring to the general idea of the subject being thought of, not each individual component.

Here's an example.

> *When I go to the store, I need to remember to get more coffee.*
> *Maybe I'll try a different kind of coffee.*
> *Oooh, maybe I'll get a flavored coffee this time.*
> *I wonder if there's a flavor like the one I had at that café?*
> *What friend did I meet at that café again?*

A train of thought like this happens within six and a half seconds. This is how easily thoughts can run away. And this goes on all day, every day in your brain. In fact, research psychologists believe this happens from the moment the brain is developed in the womb (according to a healthline.com article) until the moment you die.[2] For me, unfortunately, it happens until the moment I try to talk to women. Then my thoughts become static and amplifier feedback.

My lack of social skills aside, all that noise up there in your noggin—racing thoughts, random memories, imagining what might happen in the future, ruminating on what happened in the past—it's going to impact how you feel at any given moment.

So what does brain noise have to do with meditation? Well, only everything! Meditation gives us a fighting chance to quiet the noise and make a change

---

About," Healthline Media, medically reviewed by Jacquelyn Johnson, February 28, 2022, https://www.healthline.com/health/how-many-thoughts-per-day.

2   Researchers Scan Brain of Dying Patient: Here's What they Found https://www.healthline.com/health-news/researchers-scan-brain-of-dying-patient-heres-what-they-found

in ourselves—to become self-aware. Self-awareness isn't just about knowing "who you are." It's about recognizing when your thoughts shift, and why.

Your level of self-awareness directly affects how you *choose* to respond to certain situations.

Self-awareness allows you to choose how you respond, rather than have a flinch reaction.

Here's a simple example using the physical body. When a doctor knocks below your knee with that little hammer, your leg moves. It's a reflex, meaning the conscious mind isn't involved in the movement. Conversely, if the doctor asked you to stretch out your leg, you'd consciously choose to do so. It is a response to the doctor's request.

Here's the cool part. While we can't change how our body reacts to certain stimuli, we can change our mental responses to situations. We can ask ourselves why we're feeling a specific emotion.

Why did you get pissed off when you were cut off in traffic? Maybe you were remembering that time your date left during a movie and didn't come back. *Why didn't she come back? I thought things were going well. Good thing I don't have to see her again. Who would do that?* Then you're cut off, and so is your train of thought. Already ramped up as a result of that twenty-five-year-old memory, you have a temper tantrum in the car.

This is where I'd generally find myself throughout the day—constantly lost in memories that pissed me off and then taking out my emotions on the people around me.

When we're able to catch our mind's knee-jerk reaction, we can choose how best to respond. Maybe instead of choosing to respond to being cut off by yelling, you have a moment of gratitude because nobody was hurt and nothing was damaged.

The more you practice being aware of your reactions, the easier it becomes to reach a quieter state of being. Meditation can give us the mental space to break up that inner chatter, even for just a moment.

It's through quieting the mind that we get to truly discover ourselves—without judgment.

SO REALLY. WHY *FUCK THIS*?

Because I was tired. I was tired of being angry all the time. I was tired of being irritable all the time. After the accident, I looked at my life and thought about how much of it I'd spent being upset about dumb shit that didn't matter. I wanted to live my life, not spend it being pissed off.

And so I said "fuck this" to not having control of my mind.

I was finished sleeping with the TV on to drown out the "voices in my head," aka my runaway thoughts. I was finished with not being able to manage these thoughts. I was finished with not being able to sit quietly with myself. The final straw involved my mom and my dog, Spoons.

I was dropping off Spoons at a vet appointment, and my mom came along for the ride. While waiting in the car for our vet tech to come out and get Spoons (it was COVID-19 times), I watched other patients being attended to—patients who'd arrived after we had. Finally, while watching a chatty client occupy one of the techs, I lost my cool.

"You can wait here!" I screamed at my mom. "I'll walk home!" We were well over a mile from the house, and at this point, I'd barely walked one hundred yards in one go since the accident. I'd lost all perspective.

I apologized to my mom for days afterward, even after she told me to stop and that she forgave me. While meditating the same day as my mom's forgiveness I decided, barring horrific circumstances I would never have an outburst like that again. Not to my family, not to friends or co-workers, not to strangers, and not to myself. I had to get my irritability, frustration, and temper under control. I had to calm down my thoughts. Just as my extreme tantrum in the car was childish, off-putting, and all-around unacceptable, so were the small outbursts I was having consistently throughout the day, every day.

HOW ABOUT YOU?

Think about the last time you lost your cool. Maybe it was when neither end of a USB would connect? When you get disconnected from a call after waiting on hold for forty-five minutes? When some schmuck didn't hit the gas pedal immediately after the light turned green? "It's a green light, asshole! LET'S GO!"

When was that for you? Was it a year ago? A few months? A week? Was it ten minutes ago? In my case, everything pissed me off all the time.

You might say, "Yeah, but I am the way I am." If you think you simply have "no control" over your reactions or yourself, then I say unto you, my friend,

You are full of shit.

And I know this because I, too, was full of steaming shit. I was an angry, tantrum-throwing, door-slamming, steering-wheel-punching asshole.

"I am what I am."

Yeah? Well, I have some unfortunate news. Nobody likes adult babies. The people around you don't like your tantrums. Coworkers walk on eggshells around you because nobody wants to deal with your outbursts. Contrary to your beliefs, you don't look like a badass, you look like an asshole. Just like I did. But I have good news as well! You can live a life where you go into a frustrating situation and come out the other side not pissed off.

It all comes down to being in the moment.

Being in the moment is what allows you to see the world from a different perspective. To see that you have far more control than you realize. For me, it all boiled down to a simple sentence that I'll share with you later in the book.

First, I need to paint a picture—a landscape of how developing my self-awareness made a difference in my life.

THE ANGRY CHEF

This is the story of how a little Jewish boy from Gainesville, Florida, turned into a vulgar, fry-slinging, motorcycle-riding, metalhead chef. And then became a meditating, self-help-book-writing ninja (who's also still a vulgar metalhead).

The story begins with fourteen-year-old Josh. My folks agreed it was time for me to get a job, and my dad knew the owner of a local restaurant. He asked if they were hiring. Maybe food prep or dishwashing? It turned out they needed someone for a prep position in the mornings.

I was ready to work hard and make money. I wanted to soak up everything I could from the experience, and I ended up learning a lot: What it meant to be reliable. How to measure by volume versus by mass. How to use equations to increase or decrease recipes by percentages. How to use a knife safely. Real skills and lessons that would help me down the road. It was also at this job that I met a woman who told me that the meth she and her husband cooked was so good it would make "my dick hit the floor." Real-life experiences, that's for sure. Through and despite it all, my interest in kitchen life grew.

A couple of years later, now a junior in high school, I was introduced to a culinary program in Gainesville run by Chef Billie DeNunzio, or Chef De to her students and friends. She's led many culinary and front-of-house students to victory at regional, state, and national competitions. Many students of Chef De have found a future with a steady career that might otherwise not have had one—including me.

One day I walked into Chef De's office while she was on the phone. As I entered, she looked at me, smiled, and said to the person on the other end of the line, "I've got just the guy. I'll send him your way now." Then she hung up and said to me, "You're going to Steve's Café. They need someone."

After a quick interview with the owner of one of Gainesville's nicest restaurants, I was asked to return that evening. I'd be responsible for the salads, cold appetizers, and desserts. I had to learn how to make each component of each salad, and how to build each salad. How to make the chocolate soufflé and creme brûlée and roll out bread. I was also given the shit prep work that the other cooks were tired of doing themselves: Peel, cut, cook, and mash twenty-five pounds of potatoes for Aaron. Peel and devein shrimp for Matt. Build rosemary chicken skewers for Rich.

Along with the new-guy jobs came the new-guy pranks and teasing. I once worked for forty-five minutes in an open kitchen unaware that half my face was covered in soot. My fellow cooks' fun was ruined when a server asked me what the fuck was on my face and then suggested I go to the bathroom and clean up. Sometimes I'd be sweeping at the end of the night and one of the other cooks would promptly wipe all the junk off their station onto the floor and laugh and laugh. Then there was the towel-popping, messing with my drink, teasing me about how long it took me to do everything and about how poorly I accomplished the tasks.

That's the way it was. I wouldn't change a thing about it. Because it wasn't just industry "etiquette" and culinary techniques I was learning—it was a whole new culture. These people and the stories they told helped me transform into one of them. I was developing as a cook and a person. And I liked whom I was becoming.

These guys were funny, good with women, and intelligent. And they got angry. They'd slam and throw things. "Mother fuck" this and "Go fuck yourself" with that. It was pirate-rockstar energy. It was madness, both scary and brilliant. These were my people. At the age of sixteen, I knew this was it. This was going to be my life and there was no way around it. I'd found my passion.

And so I did what all wannabe chefs do. I worked, I studied, I bled, I sweat, and I bled a lot more. The industry consumed me. After high school, I went to the Arizona Culinary Institute, cooked at a golf resort just outside Scottsdale, and then moved to Washington. I constantly met new cooks and chefs and continued mutating into a quick-tempered, filthy-minded gentleman. Several moves and jobs later, I found myself in Tampa, Florida.

TO-SHIN DO

The move to Tampa played an important part in my future not just as a chef, but also as a person. While the reason I moved to Tampa didn't work out, I stayed for the things that did: a career-changing job and Quest Self-Defense, a martial arts dojo/school that taught "real-world self-defense" and that focused on a style I was unfamiliar with when I joined—*To-Shin Do* (pronounced toe-shin dough).

To-Shin Do is based on body positioning, bone alignment, and centuries of traditional ninja practice. Today, the ninja is typically thought to be a fictional character created by storytellers for movies. I assure you, they are real, as are the skills they've acquired over generations.

Using battle-tested techniques and principles, Master Mark "Sentoshi" Russo (the highest-ranking To-Shin Do practitioner in the world) cultivated this style to be what it is in Tampa.

He and Master Helen "Jotoshi" Russo, the highest-ranking female practitioner of To-Shin Do in the world, along with the school's lead instructor, Brodie "Ryutoshi" Mahon (now a master as well), run one of the best, most practical self-defense schools I've seen.

They teach people how to handle real-life confrontations—those situations where talking, walking, or running your way out won't work. More important than the training on the mats, though, are the seminars and private tutelage for those who want to make positive changes in their lives.

Using Buddhist teachings, psychology, and general awareness principles, Sentoshi helps people navigate their lives from a different point of view. From him, I learned about the triple secret or San Mitsu. The triple secret is the understanding that we create our reality through our thoughts, our words, and our actions. Awareness of our thoughts can influence our words, which in turn influence our actions, thus creating our reality.

Thanks to the beauty of To-Shin Do and Sentoshi's life coaching, I knew I'd found the place I was meant to be.

CRUSHING IT

Meanwhile, I was working as a sous-chef at a performing arts center that boasted a massive catering operation. The job was cool but wildly stressful. We cooked for living legends, many of whom I got to meet. Our team was responsible for building and executing menus for the performers' breakfasts, lunches, dinners, and snacks. Sometimes we fed a one-man show, sometimes an eighty-person troupe. We also catered weddings, graduations, quinceañeras, bar and bat mitzvah parties, and political gatherings. I was proud of the work we did.

Within eight months of my being hired, the executive chef left. It was quite the gut punch, as I'd been having a great time working with the guy and we complemented each other well. Both my team and office management encouraged me to take over the role. I accepted and was rewarded with sleepless nights, anxiety, panic attacks, a constant desire to quit, and a surprisingly large amount of fresh gray hair. And that was just the first week.

I spent three years at the center, and during this time I was constantly cooking, writing, and costing menus, helping in the dish pit for hours after dinner service, and brainstorming with staff to see how we'd pull off yet another impossible week.

I was regularly working eighty to one hundred hours a week and spending up to three hours a day commuting. The longest week I clocked was one hundred and twenty-four hours, not including travel. I finally hit my breaking point when the catering director came to me at the end of our busy season to tell me the "good news"—the following season had already been booked, with 10 percent more jobs.

"This team is already stretched so thin," I said. "How are we supposed to do more?"

"You'll figure something out" was the answer.

Between the impending doom of the season to come and a not-so-well-digested comment I received earlier in the season from HR regarding my team, I decided it was time to get my life back and get out of that place before it killed me. At this point, I had been a student at Quest Self-Defense for 3 years (but not training because of work) and received life coaching from Sentoshi for almost a year. It was through learning meditation, and developing self-awareness that I realized I had to make a change. I wasn't getting to enjoy my life or even the fruits of my labor.

My next and last kitchen role was as the executive chef at a hospital. I felt that my career had led me down this path for a reason. I wanted to help people, and I now had the chance to offer what might potentially be someone's only source of comfort while in the hospital, as a patient or a family member. Sadly this promising opportunity turned out to not be what I had been led to believe.

I'd spent twenty-plus years developing into the chef I'd dreamed of being. I had the skills and the knowledge. But one big skill I didn't have was impulse control. I just could not keep my temper under control. In every job I'd worked, I'd had multiple disciplinary actions taken against me. HR *loved* me, I assure you. Whether I was punching tables or walls, stabbing knives into butcher blocks, throwing things, or hurling horrendous expletives, I left my physical and emotional imprint in every kitchen I entered.

And then my career came to an abrupt halt.

THE ACCIDENT

In November 2019, I went on a motorcycle trip with my dad and his riding buddies. The vacation was just what I needed to clear my head. I'd been wrestling with whether to stay or leave the company I was with while working at the hospital. It was a decision I wouldn't get to make for myself.

On the morning of my trip back to Tampa from Gainesville, I had coffee with Mom and Dad, and Mom and I said our typical goodbyes, complete with a Josh Hug (proven by science to be the best—it has healing properties).

"Love you, honey," Mom said. "Ride safe."

"Always do."

Then I gave Dad a hug. "Had a really good time. We'll have to do this again for sure."

This was followed by one more hug for Mom, as per tradition.

Helmet on, jacket zipped and buttoned. Throw a leg over that gorgeous matte white Indian Chieftain motorcycle. Time to start the two-and-a-half-hour ride home. US Route 41 is a great ride if you're not in a hurry. It runs through undisturbed Florida wilderness and small towns. The best part was that I could get on Route 41 South and ride it almost to my front door.

The weather made for a perfect day to ride. Early in the trip, I stopped for gas, and as I filled up, I thought, *Maybe I'll take off the helmet for the rest of the ride—it's so nice out.* I loved feeling the wind whip across my face and through my hair when I rode. But for some reason, that day, I decided to keep the helmet on. Gut instinct, maybe? Regardless, it's unquestionably one of the best decisions I have ever and will ever make.

Ten minutes later, back on the road and headed south, in the amount of time it takes to say "FUCK," as quickly as you can, I was broadsided. My aggressor was a sizable northbound pickup truck turning left. The driver had been attempting to sneak between the car in front of me and the car behind me. He hadn't seen me riding between the two vehicles.

The following was pulled from the journal I kept during my rehab. I wrote this recount of the accident for legal purposes, thus the "formal" writing (it's also been tweaked slightly for polish).

DAY OF THE ACCIDENT

On November 26, 2019, I was returning home to Lutz (North Tampa) following an uneventful five-day motorcycle trip with my dad and some friends. I was riding on SR 41 South, and it couldn't have been a clearer, more-perfect day to make the ride. I was wearing full riding gear (Kevlar-lined riding pants, riding shoes, an armored jacket, a heavy riding vest, DOT-approved full-face helmet, and prescription glasses).

While in traffic moving approximately 55 mph near Dunnellon, a truck traveling in the opposite direction turned left across my lane. As soon as I noticed the truck making the turn, I swerved, attempting to evade the collision. Unfortunately, the driver didn't stop and the truck hit me on the left side. I was immediately thrown from the bike and then rolled on the ground at least half a dozen times before coming to rest. In the time between being hit and coming to a stop, I believed I was in the process of dying. I can still remember the sound of my screams reverberating off the inside of my helmet.

Once I realized I could feel sensations throughout my body, I felt it was safe to take off my helmet so I could breathe more easily. At that point, people started gathering. One gentleman was helping me calm down and gain control of my breathing so I wouldn't pass out or go into shock. I could feel that the back of my hand was hurt (it had been cut and ultimately required surgery), my wrist was in a great deal of pain, and my left leg was most definitely injured, although, at the time, I didn't know how badly. I could hear someone behind me screaming and crying. I was able to lift my head to look back. It was the driver of the truck, panicking, believing he'd just killed someone. Another person approached and said they'd already called 911 and assured me an ambulance was on the way. I asked for water and if someone could bring me my phone so I could call my parents to let them know what had happened. My dad answered.

"Hey, bud, what's up?"

"I was just in an accident."

"Oh my god, are you okay?"

"No, my leg is hurt pretty bad."

I told him the ambulance was on its way, and my dad stayed on the phone with me until the paramedics arrived. I gave the phone to one of the first responders, who told my dad they'd be taking me to Ocala Regional Hospital Trauma Center. They put me into the ambulance and radioed ahead to the hospital to describe the injuries.

When we arrived, I was rushed to the ER. At this point, the pain in my leg and foot was so bad I believed it was the worst pain possible. I could hear my parents being led into the room, and I apologized to them for putting them through this. Then a doctor said that he was sorry—he was going to have to reset the leg. The sensation of him picking up my foot and leg alone was unimaginable. But when he started setting the bones in alignment . . .

To this day, when nurses and doctors ask me, "On a scale of 1 to 10, what's your pain level?"

I consider THAT moment 10. Nothing I've ever experienced has come close to it. I believe that around that time, they started to administer beautiful pain medications. I didn't lose consciousness during or immediately after the accident. Nor on the trip to the hospital. But once they started pushing meds, my memory becomes a bit foggier.

As it turned out, the immediate issue to be resolved was a lacerated spleen requiring emergency catheterization and embolization (Google it) to stop the internal bleeding. The next surgery was on my left tibia, which was comminuted (aka "broken in more than one place") and required an intramedullary rod and about half a dozen screws. A doctor opened my foot, but due to the swelling, at that point, he couldn't do much more than clean out the wound. It would be over a month before the swelling went down enough for him to reconstruct the majority of my foot.

I recall waking up from surgery and a nurse explaining where I was. Though I was thirsty, I was allowed only small sips of water from a sponge on a stick. I also remember the doctor coming in and telling my parents and me about the damage to my foot. It was described as "a mess with nerves, bones, and tendons all over the place." Thankfully, he also said, "We were able to save the foot and even the two smaller toes, which were almost completely amputated."

For a guy who'd spent most of his life avoiding doctors because they're the ones with the needles, I was getting a "crash course" in being a patient. I was dealing with pain, fear, and stress on a level I'd never experienced. There were hands everywhere—poking, prodding, cleaning, adjusting, and hoisting.

And everybody said the same thing: "Try to relax."

Try to relax? In a hospital bed. Where you don't know what's happening and you're surrounded by masked strangers. You can barely breathe because you have broken ribs. You can't see clearly. Your wrist is throbbing. Your leg and foot are so swollen and discolored they don't even look real. You have no concept of time—shit, you don't even know if it's night or day. You're only able to lie on your back. For some reason, your right eye doesn't want to open. Every hour you need a new towel and bedsheet because you keep sweating through everything. There are tubes and machines everywhere, and they're all hooked up to you.

"Try to relax," they say.

Finding a way to relax quickly became an all-day, every-day struggle.

VASO-DOWNING

The human body is capable of a wondrous thing called vasovagal syncope, also known as vasovagal response and, by hospital staff, vaso-downing. Essentially, it's when you faint in reaction to stress—a result of a sudden drop in heart rate and blood pressure.

It's quite miraculous, really, and it's different for every person. What triggers mine is having a needle in me and feeling it moving.

Typically, a person about to vaso-down will feel light-headed or woozy. One friend told me that when it happened to them, they felt "kinda funny" and then their vision went white. The next thing they knew, they woke up on the floor.

I, on the other hand, try to fight it and maintain consciousness.

I can always tell when I'm having an episode because I get this electric tingling in my nose. This is generally the point when people pass out, I'm told. Instead, I go into phase two. My body breaks out in a cold sweat. Next, that electric tingling in my nose makes its way throughout my body and intensifies. Finally, I no longer have the strength to lift my head or even focus my eyes. This is when medical staff shove an oxygen mask over my face and turn it up full blast and do their best to help me calm down. You should try it sometime—it's a lot of *fun*.

One occasion was especially memorable. I was being prepped for a procedure, and the staff was getting ready to place the IV. (You know, the needle that they have to put in and move around for a bit.)

"Listen," I told them, "I'm really bad at handling needles. Even worse with IVs. I spoke with the receptionist yesterday requesting that whoever is best at placing IVs do mine. I don't want you to have to deal with a two-hundred-and-fifty-pound sweaty guy vaso-downing." I hoped that using their language would show them I was serious.

"Oh, everyone here is really good."

Of course. So here we go again.

Not for the first time, I heard, "Go to your happy place, Mr. Kraft." A nurse stuck my arm and started searching for a vein. I was doing my best to breathe and stay calm. I was doing okay. And then, all of a sudden, I was no longer doing okay.

I vaso-downed so abruptly and violently that the next thing I knew, there were six people around me—one was squeezing my arm, another two were trying to hold my legs, and another was putting the oxygen mask over my nose and mouth and cranking it up all the way. Meanwhile, a nurse was wiping sweat from my face, saying, "It's going to be okay. Just breathe. Slow, deep breaths." The sixth person was the anesthesiologist, who was also talking to me: "Nobody is going to stick you, Mr. Kraft. You're okay. Just try to calm down."

Eventually, I did. And once I caught my breath, I told the nurse sitting with me, "I knew this would happen, but nobody believed me. Nobody ever believes me."

After a five-minute break, the anesthesiologist was ready to give it another go and started prodding my other arm with his finger. "Don't worry, Mr. Kraft," he said. "I'm not doing anything. I'm just looking at your arm."

Wanting to believe him, I tried to stay as relaxed as possible. *Just breathe, dude*, I told myself. *You're fine. It will all be over soon. Just breeeeeathe.*

I heard the anesthesiologist say "Here's a good one." Then my arm was wiped with alcohol.

Breathe. Don't pay attention to what's happening. Breathe, DAMN YOU!

Just then one of the nurses said, "It's too bad Jessica isn't here"—I felt the stick of the needle—"She would've shown you her boobs."

BOOBS?

The comment was enough of a distraction to keep me from vaso-downing a second time. They got the IV set and immediately started giving me some really good stuff to calm me down. I'd made it through, but the episodes were getting worse. I was getting desperate.

"Go to your happy place."

"Just breathe."

"Try to relax."

There had to be something to these suggestions. I needed to learn how to access this "happy place," so I could relax physically and mentally. And unfortunately, I was going to have plenty of opportunities to practice finding it.

Jump to another surgery, another IV. There I was, struggling to maintain consciousness. The nurse holding my sweat-covered hand instructed me to "go somewhere else" in my head.

My blood pressure was dropping quickly, and I was fading. Then it happened. In a last-ditch effort, I began to describe, out loud, what I was seeing in my imagination: "Brodie and Sentoshi are on the mat. Brodie throws a punch, and Sentoshi does a tessen and then fishtails in for a leg trap."

I was straining to envision how Sentoshi's feet would move when I heard several voices saying, "It's in! It's in and it's all over, Mr. Kraft. You did great."

I did it? I did it! I'd found it. I'd found my happy place. Not the kitchen. Not on stage with a band. The dojo. My happy place was the dojo. It was a revelation.

In preparation for the next time, I'd be stuck with a needle or someone needed to mess with my foot, I practiced visualizing being at the dojo regularly. With varying degrees of *success*, I found what I would later learn was, my first anchor. It was a good thing I figured it out before the main reconstructive surgery on my foot—because I was about to be introduced to a device known as a *Wound VAC* (vacuum-assisted closure).

IT CERTAINLY DOES SUCK

An amazing piece of technology, the wound VAC uses negative pressure over an open wound to assist with tissue regeneration. If you're interested in learning more, Google it—because this story is about why my first wound-VAC experience motivated me to go further into my happy place.

The surgery required to put my foot back together resulted in a golf ball-sized hole on the left side of my left foot. The bone was exposed. I also had four stainless-steel pins keeping the newly rearranged bones aligned, and they were sticking out of my foot—one in the side, one underneath a toe, and two in the tips of other toes.

As a fun side story, one evening I managed to kick the pin in the side of my foot all the way through so that the tip was sticking out the other side. You're welcome.

The first time the wound-VAC dressing was applied was a few days after the big surgery. From what I understood, they were about to put a sponge-type material INSIDE that divot in my foot, glue it in place, and then turn on a vacuum. I don't know about you, but I'd never felt something touching the inside of my foot before. It didn't sound ideal.

Before the staff started the application process, I took a few deep breaths and tried to prepare myself. At this point, I'd been practicing finding my happy place for a few weeks. I was feeling confident. I reached right out and found it . . .

Well, I thought I had found it.

This time, I was imagining practicing a technique called fire wedging, which requires an unusual twist of the body. It takes considerable concentration to learn it—perfect for trying to distract myself.

Before the medical staff began the process, I was offered morphine. I declined, as I'd heard that some people have a tough time with addiction to it afterward. I didn't want any part of something that good. Instead, I did my best to relax my body and remain as calm as possible. My parents were at my side, ready to help however they could.

The nurse asked if I was ready.

I took one final breath and told myself, *It can't be worse than what I've already been through.*

And I was right. It wasn't worse. But it was *shockingly* unpleasant. The moment the nurse touched the inside of the wound (foot-meat and bone!), my focus on fire wedging was interrupted and I was no longer in my "happy place." I was now in my "fuck this!" place.

Giving me the middle finger, my brain said, "Listen, Joshy, I'm gonna go ahead and disconnect control of the body. Okay? But I'm also going to keep us awake to see how this all plays out."

My left leg clenched so tightly that it began to shake and spasm. Meanwhile, my left hand was gripping my leg in desperation. The more my foot shook, the more those shiny new pins in my foot jostled. Feeling the pins shaking on the outside, while the other ends were securely fastened to bones, was unsettling, to say the least. This of course led to panicking—and shaking more. The muscle spasms quickly moved through my body. I managed to reach for my mom with my right hand. My left hand remained in a death grip on my left thigh.

Dad had his left hand on my chest and his right hand on my right leg. "It's going to be okay, Josh. Just try to relax, bud."

Through clenched teeth, I told everyone how sorry I was that I couldn't stop shaking. I couldn't calm down. I was sweating, crying, and wishing I'd just died in the accident.

When my dad asked the staff if they could give me morphine now, they said yes, and I accepted. As they pushed in the drug, the shaking eased, and they were eventually able to finish applying the dressing. All that was left was to turn on the VAC. Luckily, by then the morphine was in full swing. So when the vacuum was turned on and the sponge material was squished into my foot and lightning shot up my leg, rather than convulsing again, I merely groaned and squirmed. My body was too tired to do anything more. I was physically, mentally, and emotionally drained, and this was only the first time.

I'd need to have the dressing changed every other day for two months—to start.

HOME SWEET HOME

All in all, I spent a little over two weeks at the hospital in Ocala and then another two at a rehab facility in Gainesville. Because I had capable parents and a safe place to go, a month after my accident I was discharged and sent to my parent's house in Gainesville to continue my recovery.[3]

There I was, back in the room I'd grown up in, with a twin-size bed. Usually, the space had plenty of room for fun and activities. Now, it was filled with boxes of medical gear, a walker, a wound VAC, and bedside urinals. I was now the proud owner of a water-resistant tube that went over my leg every time I showered. And to top it off, my dad got to fulfill his lifelong dream of giving me shots. It's probably important to note, my dad is a well reputable and happily retired Interventional Cardiologist. He is by far the smartest person I know, and I could not be more grateful to have him as my father.

---

3   If it hadn't been for my parents, I would've been in the hospital for several more months. One of many reasons I'm grateful to them.

That being said, whenever he would take me to a doctor's appointment he'd always joked that he wanted to ask the tending physician if he could be the one to give me a shot. I'm sure this wasn't what he'd had in mind. He ended up sticking me twice daily for six weeks, right in the belly. Basically, my worst nightmare had followed me home from the hospital. I'm happy to say, as it turned out thankfully he was good at giving shots.

My doctors were keen to stay updated on how I was handling my preexisting depression. I had originally been diagnosed as a child as a result of a physician pulling me off ADD medication too quickly. It was then that I was introduced to the strength of *depression*. It has been a long-term struggle that I've become far too familiar with over the decades. But for some reason, the depression was being held at bay. Maybe it was the pain meds, maybe it was the head injury, but depression was giving me a break.

Then while in the rehab hospital in Gainesville, I'd been diagnosed with PTSD and a traumatic brain injury. It was bizarre—I was having trouble with basic math, vocabulary, and memory. Soon came the panic attacks. My weeks were filled with appointments (generally more than one a day): psychological therapy, physical therapy, occupational therapy, and lots more psychological therapy. Some were at my parent's house, some in town, and some at locations an hour away.

Despite all these appointments, I still had a fair amount of downtime. I could only watch TV and nap so much. Before the accident, I'd play guitar or do art projects in my free time. But because I'd had surgery on my wrist and it was still on the mend, I couldn't do either of these things. And of course, I couldn't safely cook either. Mom and I were knocking out puzzles, and Dad and I were putting together wooden models. That was about it.

And that's why three things became vital in my daily routine: online To-Shin Do classes, hypnotherapy sessions, and my deepening infatuation with meditation.

PART TWO:

THE SHIFT

A FLAMINGO, A DOJO,
AND A LINK

I started my recovery at my parents' house right around the time that COVID-19 began making the news. The dojo was soon offering its classes online. The school would email a link and students could log in and participate from the safety of their homes. Some people would turn on their cameras so they could be critiqued, but I generally left mine off. Because I was mostly just watching, I felt there was no reason for people to see me—nor did I want to be seen.

As far as physically participating, I did the best I could while sitting. I'd move my arms and rotate my spine, trying to visualize how I'd position my body if I were doing the full movement. I'd watch the instructors, studying their footwork and how they shifted their body weight, and pay close attention when they corrected other students. By listening attentively to their notes, I learned to spot faulty techniques and developed a better understanding of how the techniques worked in relation to the positioning of the body. It didn't feel as if I was doing much, but I was in fact training—at a more in-depth level than I was aware of at the time.

Then one day, Sentoshi asked if anybody would be interested in a seminar called the Dojo in Your Mind. It would turn out to be exactly what I needed. It quite literally opened me up to a new world.

THE DOJO IN YOUR MIND

Sentoshi began the online seminar by helping us get physically comfortable: sitting nice and tall; head upright; shoulders rolled back and down; hands gently resting in the lap, elbows against ribs; knees at waist height or lower. (We'll dive further into "comfy spots" soon.)

He then asked us to imagine we were part of an elite team with a private training space—a hidden location that only a select few people knew existed. In this training space, whatever we were working on would go perfectly. No matter what physical confrontation scenarios were thrown at us, our responses and movements would be just right. We were to picture ourselves moving effortlessly and without tension, moving through space without constraints based on abilities or physics. Anything was possible here. We could work with our training partners of choice—friends, relatives, or fictional characters. What mattered was that it was someone whose company we enjoyed.[4]

At this point, Sentoshi had introduced me to meditation a year or two prior. I would take a minute to try and calm my thoughts. Whether I was at home, at work, or found myself alone. Often I'd try meditating several times a day. On the flip side, I would go days without practicing. The first time I tapped into a meditative state, I was able to enjoy it for maybe one second, two at most. I had the sensation of being pulled out of my body and connecting to something bigger. I like to describe it as *overwhelming calmness*. Then, at the precise moment, I became aware of this sensation, I got excited, lost focus, and fell right out of it. But holy hell was it cool! This single experience urged me to continue my meditation efforts. I realized that that moment of calmness was only a quick peek at the door that led to a completely different reality. It was the Dojo in Your Mind seminar, that helped me open that door and see what was inside.

---

4   The Dojo in Your Mind isn't restricted to martial arts. Anyone can use visualization, for a variety of reasons. It's a powerful training method.

I learned you can build, explore, and learn in this "dojo" in your mind. You can create it exactly as you want it to be. You choose the temperature and the landscape. Is there a breeze or is the air still? What does it smell like? Is the ground covered in dry leaves or fresh grass? Pebbles or sand? Is there a staircase, and do the steps represent anything meaningful? This is your world—you build it based on how you want to experience it.

The dojo in *my* mind became a place I visited often. I began spending hours a day in my head. My parents would check on me, and when I wouldn't respond to their knocking, they'd peek inside, assuming I was asleep, only to find me sitting upright in bed, eyes closed and headphones in.

I constantly expanded the dojo in my mind. Almost every detail of my world had significance. Specific areas helped me in different ways. For example, I had a healing area where I used a three-sided cup. Three sides represent San Mitsu (the triple secret). I'd imagine filling the cup with a glacial stream that ran alongside a grassy path. Then I'd pour this healing water on my foot (or anywhere I felt aches or pains). I'd also drink from the cup to heal and cleanse my body from the inside. I had a seat made of earth, where I'd focus on pulling positive, calming energy from the natural environment around me. I had a place where I could look out over a tall ravine that was lush with green grass and purple flowers that danced as the wind blew. The first time I admired this beautiful ravine I'd created, I started crying—because it was then that I truly understood how powerful the mind's eye is.

More to our point, I was learning to focus my attention and allow my thoughts to come and go, which I'd never been able to do previously. It had always seemed as though my thoughts were simply unmanageable. The dojo in my mind was game-changing, but there was one more major piece of my meditation puzzle to be completed.

ALL FLAMINGOS, ALL THE TIME

While I was still in the hospital, my mom told me she had a friend who was a hypnotherapist and that she was wanting to meet with me after I was discharged. She wanted to help me through the next stages of healing. Ann-Marie Magné quickly became one of my favorite people, as well my first guide into the subconscious world.

In a nutshell, hypnotherapy is similar to guided meditation, but it can allow you to go deeper into your subconscious mind. For over twenty years, Ann-Marie has been using hypnotherapy to help people overcome their bad habits, chronic pain, phobias, and for some unfortunate souls the inability to talk to women. While we both agreed the skill of conversing with women is essential, Ann-Marie was quite convinced that I could benefit from her specialty as a part of my therapy.

Why not? I thought. I'd always been interested in hypnosis, and what else did I have going on? Not a damn thing.

And so, it was a go with the hypno.

Within minutes of our meeting, Ann-Marie and I clicked. It was as if we'd known each other for years, or maybe in another life. We got right to work, though she explained that as with all types of therapy, it would be important to start slowly.

Good thing, too, because it got intense. I often had physical hallucinations. For instance, one time my arms started floating. Or at least I was convinced they did. It felt as if my arms were being lifted to the point that my shoulders were pushing against my cheeks. I remember thinking, *This is some wild shit.*

When Ann-Marie brought me out of hypnosis, I asked, "Did my arms lift at some point during the session?"

She told me that they'd stayed right where they were, on the table, the entire time.

Sometimes our sessions had a direct purpose, e.g., "Why do I get so anxious when I know I have to be stuck by a needle?" Other times we'd dive deep into my subconscious and root around for a subject to explore, e.g., "Why did I explode with rage that day in the car with my mom and Spoons?"

Ann-Marie taught me how to explore the conscious world—i.e., the interactions we have with other people—and introduced me to levels of my subconsciousness that I might not have found on my own. She helped me to see that an inward journey can reveal answers to so many questions. Answers that can ease both physical and deep-seated emotional pain. During our sessions, I'd describe a situation and view it as negative, yet Ann-Marie would be able to interpret the same situation as a positive. She helped me shift the way I viewed my world—my life.

Ann-Marie's favorite bird is the flamingo, and whenever I think of or see flamingos, I remember everything she and I worked on and immediately feel calm. It's why I keep the toy flamingo she gave me in the cupholder of my car to this day. Having that flamingo with me in the car helps me to stay calm while I'm driving.

The toy flamingo led me to realize that you can imprint an item with emotion. It's why as children, we have stuffed animals. They generally give us a sense of comfort. The same goes for jewelry. I wear what I like to call a grounding bracelet. It reminds me to be in the moment, to slow down, and to keep in mind what's important.

I encourage you to find an item that reminds you that everything is going to be OK. An item that reminds you to just breathe.

All together now: all flamingos, all the time, for Ann-Marie.

THE MISLED AND THE MISUNDERSTOOD

Between working with Ann-Marie and spending hours a day in the dojo in my mind, I was meditating regularly, sometimes for five minutes at a time, sometimes for an hour. Among all the lessons I was learning, two big-picture realizations came into focus.

1. I was starting to understand meditation.

But more importantly

2. I could see where people were being misled.

Many people believe that to meditate, you must clear your mind and focus on nothingness. To achieve inner peace, you must first empty your mind of all thoughts and attachments.

Clear your mind. What? Clear your mind so you're working with a blank slate? That's nonsense, at least for people like me. Most humans are far too neurotic and scatterbrained.

Clear your mind? Not happening. There's no way to focus on nothingness. Because by thinking of nothingness, you are THINKING of NOTHINGNESS. Of course, this could be a meditation in itself, but it's not the only way to meditate.

It's because of this misconception about meditation that people will say what I used to say: "I just can't meditate. My thoughts race far too much."

To which I reply, "Yeah, no shit. You and every other person."

I believed every time my mind wandered off while I was meditating, that was me failing. It was as if my mind had a mind of its own! I couldn't stop my thoughts from getting pulled one way or the other.

I want to make this next section big and bold. Because that's how people let you know something is important. Ready?

Everyone thinks that their mind races more than everybody else's. Everyone thinks that other people have thoughts that can be more easily controlled.

Guess what. *You're not special.* Almost every person I discuss meditation with says the same thing: "Oh, I just can't calm my brain down." Or, "My thoughts are just out of control." If you've ever said something along those lines, shut up and keep reading.[5]

SO WHAT IS MEDITATION?

Meditation is two processes in action.

1. Maintaining focus on an anchor (aka focal point) while waiting for the next runaway thought.

2. Noticing when a runaway thought occurs (and it will—it always will) and then gently returning to the anchor.

Here's an example of falling away from the anchor. For this exercise, our anchor will be the wind.

You begin by focusing on the sound of the wind. You feel it blowing across your face, your hair, and your clothes. In the distance, you hear a wind chime. You remember the wind chime on your parents' back porch when you were a kid. You think about the cookouts with burgers and hot dogs. How great would it be to have a hot dog with relish, mustard, and onions right now? Of course, you'd have to have chili and cheese too, and coleslaw and baked

---

5   A note on dark thoughts. People often say to me, "I can't be left alone with my thoughts—I go to a dark place." And again I'll say, "Yeah no shit! In that respect, there's still nothing special about you." Dark thoughts are generally a defense mechanism. Our ego is on guard, trying to protect us. That's why we must learn to communicate with our ego. Be kind to yourself. More on this shortly.

bea—WAIT! Wait. What was the anchor? Oh yeah, the wind. You're listening to the wind.

That is what real-life meditation resembles. Remember, all those random thoughts can happen in mere seconds. It's being aware of them that keeps us in the moment.

Clear your mind? Of everything? I don't think so. Instead, we can approach meditation knowing that our brain is going to wander from our focal point. When we notice our mind veering away, we don't get frustrated—we smile. We smile because we're in the moment. We recognized our thoughts venturing away from our anchor. Because we recognized this, we can gently bring our thoughts back to our anchor, from which they'll eventually wander again. Smile. Bring your mind back to the anchor. Over and over.

The quicker you notice your thoughts drifting, the more in the moment you are.

Only by being in the moment can you realize that your focus has run off. Remember this.

WHAT'S SO IMPORTANT ABOUT BEING IN THE MOMENT ANYWAY?

Being in the moment brings calmness and clarity. It allows for compassion. You find love for yourself you didn't know existed. You make better decisions because you're more likely to consciously respond than to react. And my favorite benefit—you don't get irritated or pissed off nearly as much. Because In-the-Moment You can more easily see that the situation just doesn't warrant that emotional tax.

Yes, I still get frustrated. Yes, I still get mad. But much less frequently and with far less intensity. And I cool down significantly faster. In summary, here's what you can expect to experience when you practice meditation and get in touch with the moment (feel free to substitute "pissed off" for whatever emotion is relevant to you):

- Get pissed off less often

- Get less pissed off when pissed off

- When pissed off, go from pissed off to not pissed off faster

What I believe I'm describing here is more commonly referred to as "happiness." If you're no longer preoccupied with being pissed off, what cool stuff might you get to enjoy? Might you be . . . happy?

Let's take a quick step back and discuss a comment I made earlier about *fry-slinging*, to shed some light on how getting pissed off is generally a knee-jerk reaction. As mentioned, I used to be the executive chef of a big catering operation. One evening, everything was utterly fucked. Numbers were wrong, orders were wrong, and people kept moving tables. We'd just sent out the third "last dinner plate."

I was cleaning up with my team and about to put a bag of fries away. Just as I opened the door to the walk-in freezer, I heard someone say that one more vegetarian dish was needed. Of course, we'd already served all our vegetarian dishes, plus the overage portions we'd had ready just in case. Well, that was enough for me. Rather than taking a breath to ground myself in the moment, calmly putting away the fries, and then figuring out how best to solve the problem, I did the following.

"MOTHER FUCK! These dumb FUCKS! Son of a BITCH!" (And this is the edited version.)

This knee-jerk vocal reaction was accompanied by my hurling the bag of fries into the freezer as hard as I could. It hit a rack and the bag ripped open.

Fries flew everywhere. Too pissed off to care about the mess I'd just made, I stormed out of the cooler. And within those mere seconds, I'd been reacting, the situation had been resolved.

That was me on a semi-regular basis. What's worse is that my attitude wasn't confined to the kitchen at work. I overreacted at home, in the car, and on the phone. I was constantly riding that edge of frustration, irritability, and anger. It was exhausting.

Luckily for us, getting in touch with the moment (and being able to consciously respond to situations) genuinely starts with one single breath. And that, my friends, is exactly what we're about to explore.

PART THREE:

THE PRACTICE

GETTING STARTED

FIND YOUR GUIDE

If you don't have much (or any) experience with meditation, I highly recommend using a guided meditation. To say it's easy to fall away from your focal point would be a gross understatement. It's to be expected and planned for.

Your brain is programmed to stay on guard. It's going to fight you every step of the way. When reprogramming our brains, we must be gentle and patient. Your brain doesn't want to get in touch with the moment. It prefers to be in its "doing" state rather than its "being" state. It will travel to the past and the future, and fiction from reality. Let a guided meditation speak over that inner chatter and monologuing. Guided meditations are ideal to help you practice maintaining focus.

It's important to find the right guide for you. You have to find the one that makes your brain go "aww yeaaah." Here are three aww-yeaaah categories to consider when trying a new guided meditation.

- Voice

- Intention

- Music/background sounds

VOICE

For me, the voice has the biggest impact (generally because I find most people annoying). Even if you're not as big of an asshole as I am, this process can take time. Don't give up. The payoff is worth it.

Be picky. See what you like. There are tons of people out there posting guided meditations. I tend to lean toward lower-toned individuals who have a light breathiness to their voices. You'll know the voice when you hear it. Maybe you like the pitch or frequency, or how softly the person speaks. Or perhaps something about their voice reminds you of someone you love. You'll feel a sensation of calm and relaxation. That's the "aww yeaaah."

On the flip side, maybe the guide makes a noise with their tongue that bothers you. Or maybe you don't like how they pronounce a certain word. Think of it this way—you could be listening to an amazing story, but if the person telling it has an obnoxious voice, the chances of you finishing that story are much lower. I wasn't able to listen to one person because of how they said "calm." The speaker's inflections, tones, and rhythms influence the experience as much as the words themselves. It all makes a difference.

INTENTION

The intention, or theme, of each guided meditation, should align with how you want to feel. For instance, if you're looking for a quick, reinvigorating meditation at work before an important meeting, you can find one that will perk you right up and get your brain ready. But I wouldn't suggest choosing a meditation like this if you're wanting to fall asleep.

You might want to set a specific intention for your day. Maybe it's physical—"I want to improve my posture"—or perhaps it's mental—"I want to be a better listener in conversations today." Hell, maybe you want to be a better lover.

There are meditations out there for every situation you can imagine. Every situation. Make sure they align with what you're looking for.

I generally stay away from meditations that contain religious references or terminology and stick with nondenominational guides. But that's just me. Listen to your gut. If something about the meditation turns your stomach for whatever reason, abandon it and move on. There are far too many options, so don't settle. You may find that you like different people for different intentions. It's your world—find your narrator.

BACKGROUND SOUNDS

The background sounds can also change your experience of meditation drastically. I like soft, windy sounds combined with slowly shifting tones. All music has its place in meditation, but when you're starting, I suggest keeping the background sound and music calm. This will help you stay focused.

BECOMING YOUR OWN GUIDE

Self-guided meditation is exactly what it sounds like—a meditation in which you lead yourself. When I do self-guided meditations, I generally speak to myself as if I'm guiding a group, using the pronoun *we*. Again, whatever works for you. I strongly suggest finding background music or noise you enjoy when you first start a self-guided practice. Going straight from a guiding voice to nothing but your thoughts can be incredibly difficult. It's also a good idea to have headphones to help block out distractions.

Find a YouTube channel, fire up a playlist on your phone, put on a CD—whatever has your aww yeaaah music—breathe, and have fun.[6]

---

6   You might try using an instrumental track that lasts more than an hour. Starting the track when you close your eyes and then pausing it when you finish makes for a great way to see how long you were meditating.

And remember, self-guiding is difficult. When you try it, don't be hard on yourself if you don't maintain focus. Practice, practice, practice. Think of your brain as a muscle that you're strengthening.

FIND YOUR COMFY SPOT

We've all seen the pictures of people sitting cross-legged, elbows resting on their knees, thumbs to middle fingers. It makes for a great photograph, but if I sit cross-legged for more than about thirty seconds, my feet and legs start to buzz, and fall asleep. So find a *comfy* position.

The goal is to keep the body "out of the way"—to find a position where we're not physically distracted. When we meditate, it's important to have steady blood flow to all extremities. We don't want parts of our bodies (or our mind) falling asleep. A tingling limb will only distract us from our focus.

Where you are right now, try sitting completely still. When you close your eyes, do you feel the need to shift? Do you feel any tingling or buzzing sensations in your legs or hands? Is your lower back starting to get uncomfortable? These are all little ways our body can distract us. That's why you need to take the time to find what works best for you.

I prefer a chair with a back and armrests, which are great for keeping my elbows in place. If my arms were in a position where they could fall, I'd have to maintain a certain awareness of them. We want to forget we even have arms, hands, legs, and feet. We want to detach as much as possible from our physical selves. My chair must also be as still as I intend to be, which means it can't swivel or bounce.

Once you've found your ideal spot, "sit up nice and tall," just as Mom used to say. Feel your spine elongate. I like to imagine someone lifting my head by the hair. No slouching. Allow your head to feel light.

Next, gently pull your shoulders back and down— don't pull so hard that you give yourself a cramp. Rest your elbows comfortably against your ribcage. You want your hips at the same height as your knees or higher. Again, this is for blood-flow purposes. You don't want your legs falling asleep. If you're in an upright chair, adjust your legs so that the bottoms of your feet are flat against the ground (unless you're one of these people who can sit cross-legged—you go ahead and sit however you want).

"But what about my hands, Josh? What do I do with my hands?"

Finding a comfortable hand position also requires some playing around. To learn about classic hand positions, Google "mudras." For now, let's start with palms up. Left hand in right? Right hand in left? Which do you prefer? I place my right hand in the palm of my left, simply because it's most comfortable for me. Allow the pads of your thumbs to rest against each other. The touching of thumbs is how we'll "close the circuit," to make sure we're tuned in to ourselves. (It doesn't need to be thumb to thumb. It can be any finger to any finger.)

Now that we've found our seated position, we're going to dive a bit deeper physically.

FIND YOUR BODY

Are your muscles relaxed? We're going to start at our feet and slowly work our way to the tops of our heads.

Begin with your toes. Are they tense and gripping the ground? Let those little piggies relax.

Next, feel the arches of your feet. Are they pushing your toes into the ground? Let them soften and melt.

Are your calves pulling or pushing? Are your quads or glutes working to keep your legs in a certain position? Release it all. With every exhale, let the tension out.

Work your way up to the hips. Are they tucked underneath you, or are they tilting forward, making your back curve? Are you sucking in your gut or trying to puff out your chest? Let all that relax—we're not trying to impress anyone here.

Keep your shoulders back and down. Feel your biceps and triceps fall limp. Allow your forearms and hands to get heavy. Feel your wrists and fingers settle into their relaxed, comfortable position.

Next, flow up the back of the neck to the top of your head and down the front of your face. Notice whether there's tension in your forehead and cheeks. It's amazing how much tension we hold in our facial muscles. Take the time to feel your face truly relax and let go.

Finally, my key to full-body relaxation: relax the jaw and the tongue. Those muscles work hard all day—talking, eating, laughing, smiling, dodging murderous teeth. While meditating, we don't want our mouths open because this takes muscle power. But we also don't want our top and bottom teeth touching because this too takes muscle and conscious effort to maintain.

To find your jaw's neutral position, situate your mouth so that your lips are loosely closed and your bottom and top teeth aren't touching. If you consciously relax your jaw, it's difficult to have tension elsewhere. The same goes for the tongue. I often notice my tongue pushing into the roof of my mouth or the back of my teeth. Allow your tongue to rest comfortably on the floor of your mouth.

This quick once-over can help us physically prepare for meditation.

FIND YOUR WAY BACK TO THE ANCHOR

Remember, we're all human beings (at least I'm pretty sure). Being human has conditions. Our minds race. So it's vital that when we meditate and our minds begin to wander, or that inner monologue gets going, we're prepared—we don't just accept that it happens but expect it to. We work on reining in that runaway horse that is our thoughts.

I'm going to make this next part big and bold. Because as we've agreed, big and bold means we're serious.

WE DO NOT GET UPSET OR FRUSTRATED WITH OURSELVES WHEN OUR MINDS WANDER.

A psychologist once told me that when exploring your past, you should be as gentle with your current self as you would be with a four-year-old version of yourself. You wouldn't look down at your adorable, smiling little face, stare into your eyes, and say, "You're stupid and worthless." Right? If you saw that child not succeed on the first try, you'd encourage them. You'd help them back up and push them to keep trying. And you would smile as you watched them try again.

This is the level of compassion we should be showing ourselves throughout this process and our life.

Getting frustrated will only make continuing a meditation session more difficult. Instead, when your mind starts to wander, gently remind yourself, "I can think about that later. Right now, I'm focusing on my breath" (or whatever your anchor might be).

If your mind starts bringing up the past, remind yourself, "That was then. This is now. Right now, I'm focusing on my breath."

Perhaps your mind wants to create a story about what may or may not happen later. Remind yourself, "That's in the future. This is now. Right now, I'm focusing on my breath."

Each time your mind wanders or the inner chatter starts, notice you've drifted from your focal point, smile, and then gently bring your attention back to your focal point/anchor.

I cannot stress this enough: **negative emotions will make reaching your desired state of meditation exponentially more difficult, even impossible**. That's why we're gentle with ourselves. On those days you can't seem to make it through even one moment of a breath without your mind wandering, come back to it later. It's okay. People who meditate consistently will tell you that some days are more difficult to wrangle your thoughts. The key is to not get upset with or judge yourself. Smile. Meditation is life-changing, but it can be abandoned quickly. Stick with it. It's not easy, but it's simple.

And hey, try to enjoy yourself.

Next up, let's take that breath, shall we?

AND NOW FOR THE MAIN COURSE

One more reminder of an important concept before we get into the exercises.

WHAT'S THIS *ANCHOR* THING AGAIN?

An anchor, or focal point, is the center of our attention when we meditate. It's what we return to when we catch our thoughts running away. For instance, in many of the exercises that follow, the breath will be our anchor. In the example I gave earlier, the wind was the anchor.

The anchor is a representation of the moment. The intention during meditation is to be consciously part of every moment. As our mind wanders off, we recognize it's doing so and then gently bring ourselves back to our anchor. We clear away the inner chatter and reconnect with the moment.

When we're connected to the moment or as I described as an *overwhelming calmness*, we can explore our subconscious. When we can sit for periods without inner monologue, we can learn to reflect without judgment. It's this clarity of mind that leads us to self-discovery and self-compassion.

Now for the exercises.

ONE SINGLE BREATH

Okay, so we've found our comfy position, and our bodies are relaxed. We're ready for a nice, long, mind-emptying meditation. Right?

WRONG! Why aren't you paying attention? Emptying our minds isn't what we're shooting for. And we're going to start with just one breath.

The point of this breath is to bring all your attention to the inside of your nose. As you breathe, feel the air passing in and out of your nostrils. Try to keep your focus entirely on that feeling.

That's it.

Simple.

Excited? Here we go! I suggest reading the following section at least three times before going for it.

THE BREATH

Start by taking a few quick, short sniffs through your nose, as if you're a dog searching for a scent.

Pay close attention to and feel the air being pushed and pulled through your nostrils.

Once your attention is on the inside of your nose, close your eyes.

Take a few more quick sniffs to focus even more.

Now, take a slow, deep inhale through your nose. Feel the air as it's pulled around the rims of your nostrils. Notice that the inside of your nose becomes cool from the fresh air being pulled in.

Maintaining your attention on the chilled spot inside your nose, slowly release the breath.

As you exhale, the air, now heated from your lungs, will warm the chilled spot.

When you finish the exhale, don't open your eyes right away. Let your normal breathing resume. Sit and be with the sensations you observed during that breath for a few seconds. When you're ready, open your eyes.

Sit quietly for a minute or two. If you're outside, admire the beauty of something common in nature. The color of a leaf. The trees swaying in the wind. How the air feels on your face. If you're inside, take the time to appreciate what's around you. Think about someone you care about. Or a pet and how much you love them.

Please read that two more times, to commit the process to memory.
I'll be in the other room waiting. Just let me know when you're finished.

How was that? Pretty cool, eh? If you didn't make it through that breath without your mind wandering, congratulations—you are in fact human. It takes practice to get through One Single Breath. Regardless, I'd be willing to bet you did experience something. Even if just for a moment or two. Perhaps the calm clarity that comes from being truly focused.

It's one-hundred-percent worth spending part of your day tuning in to your breath—to yourself. My life changed when I started doing this type of work, and yours just might too. Not only did I become more self-aware, but I also became more aware of the people around me, both loved ones and strangers.

When you tune in to your breath every day, you'll start to recognize shifts happening in your mind. You'll live in the moment more often.

I recommend beginning each meditation session with The Breath exercise to start tuning all of your attention inward. I then follow this with the Counted Breath, to start with "fresh" lungs. The Counted Breath isn't just a fantastic way to prepare for other meditations—it's also an anchor in itself.

THE COUNTED BREATH

In the guided-meditation world, this exercise goes by a few names, including Charging the Battery and the Cleansing Breath. The purpose is to clear out any stale air that might be sitting at the bottom of your lungs, send massive doses of oxygen to your blood and brain, and expel excess carbon dioxide.

First and foremost, never do this exercise while standing or driving. People have passed out pushing themselves too hard while learning this exercise. Always sit or lie down while practicing the Counted Breath.

Prep for the inhale
Before attempting the exercise, please read all the way to "Enjoy."

Take a deep breath. Imagine your inhale starting down in your belly and filling your lungs completely with air. Then blow the air out forcefully. Do this two to three times and then let your body's natural breathing take over. This way, you'll start the Counted Breath with fresh air.

Here's the counting part:

- Four-second inhale
- Seven-second hold
- Eight-second exhale

Let's break down each step.

THE INHALE

On the count of one, begin your inhale. Do your best to pace your breath, so you're inhaling smoothly. Use the full four seconds to take your lungs from empty to full. By the time you count to four, you should feel as though your lungs can't possibly fit any more air.

THE HOLD

Hold that deep breath in for seven seconds. In those seven seconds, let your body relax around your fully inflated lungs. Let your shoulders fall and release any tension in your arms and hands. If your face is scrunched up, let it be at ease. Notice all the unnecessary tension your body takes on when it believes you're in distress. We're learning how to recognize that tension and then let it melt away.

THE EXHALE

Control the release of your breath over the course of eight seconds. As you near the end of your count, you should be nearly straining to push any last pockets of air out of your lungs.

Inhale, hold, exhale—that's one cycle. I tend to run this cycle four times. At the end of each eight-second exhale, begin your next four-second inhale immediately. Again, pace the inhale so that when you reach the count of four, it feels as if you can't manage even one more sip of air.

Once you finish the cycles, let your natural breathing rhythm take over and bring your attention back to your nose and find your breath.

A question to consider: When you release the tension on the hold, do you notice how that tension isn't doing anything to help? Does that tension make the exercise more difficult?

The more tension we let go of, the easier life becomes.

I highly suggest spending time practicing the Counted Breath. Making that connection between your conscious mind and your lungs is a great way to get in touch with the moment. You're observing what's required to pull, hold, and then push your breath, all while releasing as much tension as possible. When we use only the necessary muscles to achieve a full cycle of the

Counted Breath, we're forced to find pockets of tension and then consciously release them.

If at some point while practicing the Counted Breath you feel the need to reset your breathing, please do so. Remember, we're reprogramming. We're putting a lot of focus into something we rarely do. If filling your lungs is a bit much, start with mostly full.

It is completely normal if you experience a "buzzing" sensation or light-headedness. Colors can sometimes become brighter or more vibrant for a few seconds. Any effects will wear off once you resume normal breathing.

Enjoy.

We've gotten a glimpse. An appetizer, if you will. We've initiated the connection between our minds and our lungs. In the next exercise, we're going to deepen that connection as well as the connection between our conscious thoughts and our breath.

THE SLOWEST BREATH POSSIBLE

Consider how long an average breath lasts (full inhale and exhale and any natural pauses). How many breaths do you think you take per minute? If you guessed between twelve to sixteen, you're right.[7] This means one cycle of breath takes roughly four or five seconds.

So I was shocked to learn that some people could inhale for one solid minute and then exhale for another minute. Wanting to try it, I figured that fifteen seconds would be a good place to start and work up from. Seemed easy enough.

My first try went something like this:

> One second
> *This is nice.*
> Three seconds
> *This is great!*
> Five seconds
> *No problem.*
> Eight seconds
> *Hmm . . . ?*
> Ten seconds
> *Exhale*

What the hell? I can hold my breath for longer than ten seconds but I can't inhale for ten seconds? And who are these people taking two-minute-long breaths?

Despite my doubts, I kept exploring what I started calling the Slowest Breath Possible. And time after time, I kept running out of air. Sometimes it was at

---

7   Johns Hopkins Medicine, "Vital Signs (Body Temperature, Pulse Rate, Respiration Rate, Blood Pressure)," the Johns Hopkins University, the Johns Hopkins Hospital, and Johns Hopkins Health System, accessed November 2, 2022, https://www.hopkinsmedicine.org/health/conditions-and-diseases/vital-signs-body-temperature-pulse-rate-respiration-rate-blood-pressure#:~:text=Respiration%20rates%20may%20increase%20with,to%2016%20bre

five seconds in. Sometimes I made it to the exhale, but then I'd have trouble controlling that. Then one day while spray-painting in my shed, it clicked.

I was about to spray a quick clear coat on a painting. Since it was going to be an in-and-out session, I decided to hold my breath rather than spend the time putting on my respirator. To prepare, I took a couple of deep breaths and then a deep breath to hold. I pressed the nozzle. As the fumes filled the space, my awareness of not being able to breathe crept in. My lungs screamed, "Why are we holding our breath? Breathe, damn you!"

Instead of stopping what I was doing to jump outside and catch my breath, I let some air out of my lungs in a thin stream—slowly enough that I could finish spraying. And I realized that what I'd thought was a desperate need for fresh air was actually my lungs panicking.

Even though my brain knew there was fresh air nearby available for wonderful breathing, my lungs weren't functioning as they were used to. By simply letting go of the tension I was holding, I was able to comfortably finish the clear coat.

My mind blown, I stepped out of the shed. Then, rather than gulping air as soon as possible, I sipped it, sending steadily paced fresh air to my now-relaxed lungs. The connection was made. It wasn't that my lungs had to get fresh air at that exact moment—it was that I was forcing them to work differently. I was reprogramming them.

There was far more to the slow-breathing exercise than I'd thought. It wasn't just about seeing how long I could make a full breath last. It was about building a relationship between my body and my mind. I could remain calm and deepen my sense of being in the moment.

Our brains respond well when we keep calm: *Everything is good. No need to panic, no need for alarm, all is well. Yes, we're breathing a little differently, but it's okay.* Not so much when we think, *OHHHHHHHH SHIIIIIIIIIIIIIIIIIIIIIIIIIIIIIT!*

The truth is, unless something is physically preventing you from doing so, your body won't let you stop breathing and suffocate. It won't happen. If you were to pass out from holding your breath, you'd start breathing again. So with that in mind, please do this exercise while sitting or lying down, and in a place where you can't fall and hit your head.

While practicing the Slowest Breath Possible, stay focused on this one breath. Your only thoughts should be, *Nice and easy. Lungs, we're fine. Brain, we're fine. Everybody just be cool.*

It's important to note that you don't have to do a full minute to get the benefits of this meditation. To this day, I can't consistently do a one-minute inhale and a one-minute exhale. My average time is closer to thirty seconds each. Don't get hung up on going for a full sixty seconds. The point is to consciously communicate with your lungs.

The next step is to see how many slow breaths you can take in a row. I find that the deeper attention I pay to my breath, the less I care about the time aspect of the exercise. Because let's remind ourselves, this is about connecting and quieting all the racing thoughts. So if you tune in and forget to click the star/stop on the stopwatch, that's a success in my book. Sometimes when my lungs start screaming for air during the exhale, if I take just a small sip of air that will calm the impulse to take a full inhale. Always take a full reset breath whenever you need to. That's part of the process. Don't get frustrated when your body truly does need to breathe. Take a moment and compose yourself. Then go again.

When you reset, use that breath to tune in. Bring your attention to the sensation of your lungs inflating slowly, from your lower belly all the way up. Then relax around that breath.

This exercise was a milestone in my meditation journey. When you send all your attention to a specific part of the body, you can pick up and learn so much—such as the fact that your lungs are simply aching for someone to tell them what's going on and that they're not in danger.

It takes time to cultivate the ability to communicate calmly, clearly, and honestly, whether it's with your mind and body or with another person. But this type of communication tends to lead to better results all around.

DO YOU SMELL THAT?

Our sense of smell is our most direct link to memory. In other words, nothing reminds you of something more than a smell. This is why it works well in a meditation exercise—it challenges us to detach.

Despite the exercise's name, it's not about pinpointing smells. It's about acknowledging smells and then detaching from them. And since we're practicing both being in the moment and detaching, here's a reminder:

**We don't allow ourselves to get upset when our
brain does what it has always done: trail off.**

When you recognize your brain wandering, smile. Noticing you're off your anchor is the entire point! You just connected to the moment. Gently bring yourself back to your breath and your original anchor for the meditation.

Now, for the exercise.

With each breath you take, you can experience multiple scents. Your brain will want to explore the memories connected with the initial smell it picks up, but this exercise is about consciously detaching from one scent and being ready to notice the next. Do *not* spend time putting a name, a description, or a source to what you smell. Once the smell passes or shifts, recognize the change and continue breathing.

There will be pockets of seemingly neutral-scented air. Take this time to connect with your breath. Feel the inside of your nose chill with the inhale and then warm on the exhale. Refresh your scent palate and return to the anchor of smell.

Keep in mind that this exercise is about detachment. You'll experience how easy it is for a smell to trigger memories or thoughts—and how fast your subconscious mind will want to explore them, pulling you away from your anchor. Here's how one moment can derail you from the moments that follow.

Let's say you're outside and it's a beautiful day, so you decide to practice Do You Smell That? You're a couple of minutes in. All is going well, and then mid-inhale, you can smell that your dog is taking a shit next to you.

Come on, man, seriously?

You pick up your chair and move it somewhere else in the yard to get back to breathing. But now all you can think about is the smell of dog shit. You end up spending twenty minutes moving your chair from spot to spot trying to get back to your breath. You're so attached to the smell of dog poop that you don't get to enjoy the smell of the perfectly cooked cinnamon rolls wafting out of your neighbor's house. At least that's how it worked out for me.

It was only while making my way inside, having given up on meditating outside, that I picked up on the cinnamon rolls. That's when I discovered this exercise. It was quite an awakening. I was so preoccupied with the gift that Spoons had made for me that I wasn't able to enjoy the smell of cinnamon rolls.

A moment can begin and end at any, well, moment. When that moment is over, all we're left with is a memory. If we put too much focus on what *was*, we miss what *is*. When we focus on negative moments that have already come and gone, we miss the good ones that come after.

As quickly as a smell can capture your attention—that's how quickly a situation can change, for better or worse.

Because of our attachment to moments, it can be easy to believe that each moment is dictated by previous ones. Maybe your laundry isn't fully dry when you need it to be. Maybe you burned the toast. Or your dog took a shit next to you while you were trying to meditate. If your day starts poorly and you, therefore, believe that the rest of your day is going to go just as poorly, you're falling prey to the Baader-Meinhof theory, also known as frequency bias.

In short, when you notice something new and fixate on it, you then seem to see it everywhere. Perhaps it's a breed of dog, or a word, or even a number. Our brains love patterns. It attaches to them, making it easy for our subconscious thoughts to find them again.

If we allow ourselves to attach to the idea that our day is about to be terrible, chances are we'll subconsciously find something terrible in everything we experience throughout that day, rather than recognize that each event is independent of the others.

Since I've started meditating regularly, most of my moments have ranged from neutral to positive. Of course, there are negative moments. There always will be. But know that when the dog shit wafts by, you don't have to be as distracted by it. After all, you don't want to miss the cinnamon rolls.

SINGLED OUT

We won't always be able to go to our perfect meditation spot, where everything is set up just right. If there's one thing we can count on, it's that there will usually be distractions. In Florida, we've got bugs, animals, Florida-Man, weather—it's never silent.

"Well, Josh, how the hell do you expect me to be able to meditate in all that racket?"

I'm glad you asked. For context, I'll tell you about a game I created. This game is aptly named the Game.

The Game was created to endure the irritations of a kitchen manager. Please note that an annoying manager isn't required to play the Game. It can involve any person you're forced to be near. We all know the kind of person I'm talking about. The person who'll tell the same joke until it's cold and dead in the ground. Or tell the same sob story to every person they pass. Or who feels the need to make comments about anything and everything.

One day while the other cooks and I were commiserating over our comedy-destroying manager, we realized he was saying the same thing to each person he encountered. I decided it would be fun to count how many times this manager repeated himself. The Game was born.

Here's how it works. The manager comes into the kitchen and tells you his new favorite joke that involves talking muffins. Perfect. He finishes his rendition of something that was once funny and walks away. You're now in the Game.

Over the noise of the kitchen, you hear him mutter, "Something something, talking muffins." You look and see that he's telling the same joke to the dishwasher. That's one point for you, and the dishwasher is now in the Game.

A server comes into the kitchen, and you see the manager run over and tell them the joke. That's another point for you, and one point for the dishwasher, and the server is now in the Game. And so on, and so on.

As a group, we went from being miserable and irritated by this guy to looking forward to seeing him coming. Everybody was smiling. At the end of the shift, nobody cared who'd tallied the most points.

The outcome of this silly idea was remarkable. The manager hadn't done anything differently. He hadn't changed his ways, nor should he have been expected to. But instead of getting pissed off or irritated, we smiled.

I used the Game in every kitchen I worked in after that. People will always be obnoxious. There's no way around that. But if we can get in touch with the moment, be aware of our thoughts, change our perspective, and show some compassion, we can change our reality. That's what the Game is all about.

"Yeah, yeah. What does this have to do with meditation?"

One day while rehabbing at my parent's place, I'd just had the dressing changed on my ever-improving foot. Still feeling the residual effects of the medication, I was especially relaxed and went outside to meditate.

I began the Counted Breath. *In for four, hold for seven, out for eight.* I did this several times before letting my natural breathing take over.

I was then audibly assaulted by the outside world. There I was trying to find my center amidst crickets chirping, cicadas buzzing, and birds making all the noises they make. Not to mention the sounds of cars and other human-made noises. It all created an erratic rhythm. I was starting to get pissed off.

I want to meditate outside, but all these damn bugs and animals and people are making too much noise!

Then, like magic, I remembered the Game. How could I change my perception? How could I shift from being irritated to enjoying the noise? I thought about how it wasn't just one cricket chirping but many, creating a singular sound. Sort of like when it's raining—you don't hear one drop at a time necessarily but all the drops hit separately but consistently. Maybe this idea of the Game could help me focus.

I closed my eyes and began to listen to my breath. As expected, the cacophony of nature's music started getting my attention. But this time, I put all my attention on what I was hearing, which was mostly crickets. I focused on the sound, concentrating on the direction it was coming from. Then something incredible happened. I was no longer hearing all the crickets. I had zeroed in on one cricket and its song. I could hear it when it started and stopped chirping. I knew if I got excited I'd be pulled away from the experience. So I got excited and got pulled away from the experience.

My frustration was quickly pushed aside by the knowledge of what I'd just done. I'd uncovered a new meditation technique for myself. The Game had won again.

Here's the process for Singled Out. To explore this exercise, let's take ourselves outside—or at least near an open window.

As always, start by getting comfy. Then comes the Single Breath. Do the little dog sniffs to bring your attention to your nose. Then a slow, deep inhale and exhale. As you let your normal breathing take over, sit with any observations you made during that breath. *Did the inside of my nose get cool when I inhaled? Could I feel the air being pulled over the edge of my upper lip? Was there still tension somewhere in my body?* After noting your observations, move on.

Take a deep, lung-filling breath in, all the way from your lower belly to your upper lungs. Hold that breath for just a second or two, try to relax your body around that breath, then let it fall away. Then, when you're ready, begin the Counted Breath.

Use the entire four seconds to inflate your lungs as much as you possibly can.

Hold that breath for seven seconds. Locate and relax any pockets of tension.

Exhale that breath for a count of eight. Use the full eight seconds to empty your lungs as much as you can. Then on the count of one, start the cycle again.

> In for four.
> Hold for seven.
> Out for eight.
> Repeat.

Once you've finished and your normal breathing has taken over, continue to mentally examine your body for any last bits of tension. Take a minute to enjoy the peaceful stillness of the moment. When you're settled in, allow yourself to listen to your surroundings.

Listen. . .

Get comfortable with the symphony provided for you. Let it fill your ears. See if you can count how many different sounds you hear. Can you hear frogs? What about birds or insects? Even if it's quiet, noise is always being made. Just breathe and listen.

From this place of stillness, see if a particular creator's sound catches your ear. As you listen, get a general idea of where the noise is in reference to your body. Is it to your left? Your right? In front of you? Behind? Here comes the bold piece:

It doesn't matter where the sound is coming from.

We're exploring *perspective*, not visual location. Let yourself be okay with not knowing for certain.

Once you have a rough idea of the sound's location, shift all your attention in that direction. Every time you hear your musician, zero in, closer and closer, until you feel you've pinpointed the location of one musical creature. Get so focused on it that you can imagine drawing a straight line from your head directly to the creator of the sound. I cannot stress this enough—do not check to see how accurate you are. Just like Do You Smell That, this exercise is about detachment and allowing yourself to enjoy the moment for what it is. It's your time to breathe and let go.

I do this exercise regularly—not just because I'm surrounded by loud little creatures, but because there's something special about hearing one out of many. You make a unique connection with nature when you focus your attention on one creator of music among an orchestra of buzzing and chirping musicians.

Note that it's possible to have auditory hallucinations, especially when you're intently focused on a sound. I once heard what sounded like a car slowly driving through my living room. I've also heard a squirrel eating behind me. I was so focused on the noise of it munching on acorns that it sounded as if it were sitting on the back of my chair, right next to my ear. It can be quite an experience.

A note on compassion

The ability to consciously change your perspective on a situation is a powerful tool. The Game isn't just a game. It's a way of experiencing our world. It's a way of life.

When you can change your perspective, you can feel compassion more easily. If we showed compassion to each other more often, so many of the problems humanity faces would be rectified. Showing compassion to another human requires the ability to show it to yourself. We'll discuss this in a little more depth later. For now, keep the idea of compassion for yourself in mind throughout the process of finding your breath.

THE PULSE OF THE FLOW

The best way to observe what happens during this meditation exercise is to sit as still as possible. To prepare for stillness, let's spend a few minutes getting loosened up in our comfy spot.

I'm a particularly antsy person, so it's difficult for me to sit still for even a couple of seconds. If you're like me, take the time to get out any last stretches, twitches, and knuckle cracks before a longer meditation. It makes sitting motionless far more comfortable.

We're going to work our way from our toes all the way to our face. Feel free to shift until you're ready to move to the next body part. There is no time limit. Spend the time you need to settle in.

Relax. Tune in.

Let's start with a big deep breath.

Starting in the belly, fill all the way up to the top of your lungs. Hold that breath for a second or two, relaxing your body as much as you can around that held breath. Then let it fall away.

Stretch your arms and hands straight out in front of you. Spread your fingers wide then make a tight fist. Do this several times. Feel the tendons elongate and relax as you release the tension in your arms. Next, using your wrists draw circles in the air with your hands. Roll them in both directions. Lastly, make tight fists once more, and then let that tension fall away from your hands.

Next, roll your shoulders forward, making big circles. After a few slow circles, reverse the direction. Try touching your shoulders to your ears as you bring them around the top of the circle. End by gently squeezing your shoulder blades back and down.

When you're ready, place your hands in their resting position: relaxed palms up, one hand resting in the other, pads of the thumbs touching, closing the circuit.

Take a deep breath.

Lifting your feet off the ground, draw circles in the air with your toes by rolling your ankles. Feel all the muscles flex and relax as you do. Then lower the balls of your feet and your toes to the ground and raise your heels. Feel your calf muscles tighten and then soften as you lower your heels. Next, keep your heels on the ground and lift the front sections of your feet. Feel the muscles on your shin flex and then relax as you lower your feet fully to the floor. Clench your toes to make little feet fists. Notice the muscles at the bottom of your feet tense then relax as you unclench your toes.

Breathe deeply. Feel the inside of your nose cool with the inhale and warm on the exhale.

Next, flex your quads and glutes. Notice how you rise in your seat when those muscles are flexed. Slowly lower your body and notice your muscles relax as you melt back into your seat.

Take a deep, deep belly breath.

Still, in a seated position, curve your spine slowly in each direction. Get out any pops or cracks. Once you're satisfied with how your back feels, keeping your spine straight, slowly lower your head to the left. Focus your attention on the stretching sensation on the right side of your neck as you do so. Then feel the muscle it takes to lift your head back upright. Repeat this process on the right, and then do the same lowering your head forward and then back. Each time, feel the different parts of your neck stretch and the muscles required to bring your head back to the center.

Deep breath. As you inhale, check to see if your shoulders are still rolled back and down. Then on the exhale, without moving, see if you can feel whether or not your hands are still seated in the desired position.

Take a slow . . . slow breath.

Send your attention to the top of your forehead. Relax your brow and cheeks. Imagine letting go of so much tension that your face begins to sag. Every facial muscle should feel as if it's melting. Finish by releasing your jaw and tongue to their neutral positions.

We're now physically prepared for a longer meditation session. Most of our jimmies have been worked out.

It's time to find our breath.

When you're ready, start with those quick sniffs and bring your attention to your nose. When you're focused, take that slow breath. Do you feel the cool spot develop inside your nose on the inhale and then warm on the exhale? Can you feel cool air being pushed or pulled over your upper lip? Allow your body to resume its natural breath as you sit with your observations of that breath for a few seconds.

Now, take a few deep, lung-clearing breaths, exhaling forcefully.

> Then the Counted Breath.
> In for four.
> Hold and relax around that breath for seven.
> Out for eight.

Three more times.

> In for four, hold for seven, out for eight.

In for four, hold for seven, out for eight.
In for four, hold for seven, out for eight.

On the final exhale, push out every bit of air. Once you feel as if you can't possibly push out any more air, let your body's natural breathing pattern take over.

Give your body a few moments to settle.

Once you're ready, let your attention ride the inhale through your nose down to your lungs. On the exhale, allow your attention to rise to the surface of your skin at the center of your chest. Can you feel the cloth touching your skin? Does your breath move your chest or stomach enough that the fabric slides or stretches around you as your lungs expand and contract? Simply observe these sensations. Observe without any form of judgment or criticism. Enjoy the calm.

With every breath, your body becomes more and more still. More comfortable being exactly where it is. In your stillness, you'll feel rhythmic pressure throughout your body. Spend a minute exploring that rhythmic pressure. When you're ready, bring all your attention back to the center of your chest. You're going to find the source of the rhythm.

Narrow your attention to the point slightly left of the center of your chest. Feel for the steady beat. Feel the rhythm of your heart pumping. The deeper your focus, the more precisely you can feel your heart working inside your chest. That rhythm is always there, sending oxygenated blood through your body. Take a moment to appreciate your heart.

Deep breath.

Keeping a sense of your heart's rhythm, send all your attention to your fingertips. Without moving, feel your hands from within. Can you find the pulsing rhythm of your heart at your fingertips? How about in the palms of your hands? It will feel like a slight inflating sensation that syncs up with your heartbeat.

You're currently experiencing something that every person can do but that most won't take the time to do. You're experiencing your heart beating. You're experiencing the moment. See if you can feel your pulse anywhere else in your body. Feet? Hips? Neck? Can you feel your heart beating in your lips?

Sit with the rhythm of your life's engine for as long as you wish.

When you're ready, take a deep lungful of air. Hold it. Relax around that breath, and then release it. One more deep, deep breath. Hold for a moment. Then let the air fall out of you. Start to bring yourself back to where you physically are. Shift around, and when you're ready, take one more deep breath and, on the exhale, open your eyes.

Sit quietly. Don't speak. Just *be* for a few moments.

I accidentally discovered this exercise while working on muscle relaxation. I'd start by picking a muscle, finding the tension there, and then consciously releasing it. I'd stick to one muscle for a while because I was noticing that even after I let the tension go, there was a little more left. In this way, I'd slowly make my way across my entire body. It was surprising how many little pockets of tension existed.

One day while focusing on my shoulders, working them down and back, I noticed tension in my upper body. Connecting to the muscles in my chest, I tried to let them soften and melt with each breath. It was then that I noticed a rhythmic pulse. The sensation was coming from inside of me. I was feeling my heartbeat. In a completely calm state, I was able to precisely feel my heart's rhythm (the lub AND dub if you will). I followed my pulse down to my fingertips, actively feeling my heart as it sent life force throughout my body. I'd never felt so close to my physical self. So in tune.

I'd finally figured out how to relax. And it was my breath that had guided me there.

RIBBON DANCING

One peaceful morning in Gainesville, I was working on the dojo in my mind. I couldn't manage to settle down enough to focus, but I was enjoying the quiet stillness of the morning. The air felt good. The sounds of nature were just right. I was physically comfortable. I just couldn't maintain focus enough to practice the meditation exercise I'd set out to. I broke my hand posture to rub my eyes.

Do you remember the last time you rubbed your eyes and your vision got a little wonky? Maybe lit-up colors and shapes exploded like a kaleidoscope behind your eyes? I'd experienced the kaleidoscopic light show at various points in my life but generally hadn't thought much of it. This time, I sat and "watched" those ribbons of light as they danced. It dawned on me. All my attention was focused on the light show.

The problem was that trying to look at the ribbons strained my eyes. The more I moved my eyes to "see" the lights, the more it hurt. Then it clicked—the visions were coming from inside my head. They weren't external. My brain was generating these images. This was the moment I understood the term *the mind's eye*. With practice, we can develop it. And just like a muscle, the more you work it, the stronger it becomes.

This was huge for me. The possibilities of visualization could be endless.

Those ribbons of light are called phosphenes, and they're caused by pressure or tension on the eye. The scientific why doesn't matter for our purposes. I like thinking that our brain prefers having something to occupy itself with, so when we're in absolute darkness, it projects these wild, flowing, geometric patterns for itself to interpret.

That's right, my friends, we're hallucinating. Again.

So what are we gonna do with this phenomenon? We're going to honor what our brain wants to do and use it as our anchor. You don't have to find a completely dark room. Just closing your eyes can bring on the light show. If you're having trouble getting the phosphenes moving, gently rubbing or tightly closing your eyes for a moment will usually do the trick.

Once they begin, give yourself a moment to appreciate what's happening. You're aware enough to consciously partake in a natural phenomenon happening in your brain! I still don't understand how people aren't talking about this all the time. **This is my go-to form of meditation when I'm having a hard time settling my thoughts.**

It bears repeating. We don't have to get frustrated quit when the meditation practice we're choosing to work on doesn't go as planned. There are plenty of great focal points. The important thing is you find your breath, even if just for a few moments.

The Ribbon Dancing exercise helped me hugely further my work with the dojo in my mind. But more importantly, it helped me create what would become my favorite meditation practice: Seamless Breathing.

SEAMLESS BREATHING

I call this exercise Seamless Breathing because the intention is to transition between the inhale and the exhale and then between the exhale and the inhale as gently and indiscernibly as possible.

The most fun part of this exercise is the visual. First, imagine you're looking at your reflection in a full-length mirror, you could be standing or sitting in your visualization. Then imagine a ball of golden light sitting on the floor just a few inches in front of you.

Now think of a clock face. Your feet are at six and your head is at twelve. The top of the clock face is where your inhale becomes the exhale. The bottom is where the exhale becomes the inhale.

The ball of light moves with your breath. As you complete an entire breath (in and out) the ball will make a full circle, from six all the way around back to six.

Here's how we put it all together.

As you inhale, the ball of light starts to lift, slowly swinging upwards to form the circle. As it reaches the top of the circle, slow your breath to almost a full stop. See the ball of light in your mind's eye as it hovers almost motionless above your head. As you slowly release your breath, the ball of light begins its descent.

When your exhale is nearly complete, slow your breath again, and bring the ball to almost a full stop. Then begin your inhale slowly and gently. Watch as the ball of golden light starts its upward climb again.

Give it a go. Find your breath and see if you can move the ball of light as smoothly as your breath.

If you managed to conjure up a ball of light, did it move jerkily? Did it race all over the place? Or perhaps it turned into someone you know? Your subconscious will fight you the whole way. It will do everything in its power to keep you from focusing on that ball of light. Regardless of how your first try went, I have fantastic news for you: it's impossible to control your ball of light right from the get-go. Shit, you can barely control it with lots of practice.

The point of Seamless Breathing isn't to visualize a ball of light that moves perfectly and smoothly. We go into this exercise knowing the ball will jump. Just as we know our minds will race. Detach from the idea that the ball will swing perfectly, and as you become aware of the derailment, smile and put it back on track. Again, and again, and again.

Seamless Breathing is about spending time with the breath. The ball of light is the anchor. The visual reminds us of what we're practicing. It reminds us that we're tuning in to our breath. That we're consciously involved in every tiny movement required to bring the ball of light full circle.

Also, keep in mind that you don't have to do the visualization while working on the breathing technique. I generally find myself sending all my attention to the back of my nose to see just how subtly I can make the transitions between the inward and outward breaths.

As is the case with all our meditation exercises, it's not about mastery. It's about practicing. You have to learn to enjoy the art of practicing. If the ball of light wants to jump around, simply bring yourself back to this idea: *It's my breath that moves the ball, not my random thoughts.* Gently reposition the image in your mind and continue the breathwork.

Don't get frustrated if you're having a tough time. It's okay. Because you know who else has had a tough time working on this? Every single person I've introduced it to, including me. It takes being in touch with the moment and recognizing that the ball jumps the way our thoughts do. The quicker we notice the ball is off course, the quicker we can put it back on track.

Mastery isn't a destination. It's a lifelong path.

THE PEN AND
ITS WISDOM

Remember earlier I told you I was going to share a simple sentence with you? It was so long ago, and we've been through so much together it may be hard to recall. Either way, here we are, the final course. The dessert you never knew about but always wanted. This is what we've been working toward—a sentence that ties directly to being in the moment.

We've looked at how meditation, hypnotherapy, and training in the dojo in my mind played a massive role in my recovery. In finding my breath, I was born anew. Had things not worked out the way they did, I very well might have lived the rest of my life letting my ego make all the decisions for me. I might have spent my life reacting rather than responding to the world around me. It all came together to open a door to self-awareness. It's this self-awareness that allowed me to understand a special sentence.

I give this pen all the meaning it has to me.

These eleven words changed how I interact with the world.

It will probably come as no surprise that it was Sentoshi who passed along this life-changing tidbit. It was at the end of one of our life-coaching sessions. I was rambling about how irritated I was getting at work (go figure). I was constantly pissed off with employees, coworkers, and myself. It felt as if each problem was building on the last, and I couldn't separate or prioritize myself. I was out of patience.

Sentoshi smiled empathetically. He asked if he'd talked about the pen and its meaning.

"No," I said, caught off guard.

He picked up a pen, held it between us, and said, "I give this pen all the meaning it has to me."

To which I replied, "Okay . . . ?"

"Do you understand?"

"I don't think so."

He laughed. "Anyone can give this pen meaning," he said. "But only I can give it the meaning it has to me."

I nodded, understanding the sentence itself, but I had no clue why he was telling me this. And so the statement floated around in my head. Eventually, I thought I got it. *It doesn't have to be a pen. It could be anything—a car, a person, this book.* I wasn't sure how this knowledge was supposed to help me at work, though. I was already having trouble with prioritizing, and now I was having trouble attributing meaning to these "pens" as well.

Several years and a whole bunch of living, including the accident, happened before the true revelation. At this point, I'd been back in Tampa for only three weeks, after recovering in Gainesville for the previous ten months. My folks and I had said our goodbyes, complete with hugs, and they'd driven away, leaving me at my home.

I soon began struggling with an overwhelming sense of being out of place. I was depressed and having panic attacks. I cried more often and was far jumpier. I was hypersensitive both physically and emotionally. It took the better part of two months to figure out the best way to describe what I was experiencing.

A brief side-story, but worth telling (Warning: I'm about to nerd out a bit).

I was feeling was similar to what Captain Jean-Luc Picard must have gone through in the episode where he's knocked out by an alien beam.[8] While only minutes pass for the crew as they watch Picard lying motionless, Picard's consciousness lives an entire lifetime—all the pain, the love, the forgiving, the acceptance. He lives and dies in this other world only to be zapped right back to the present where the ship and the crew were still dealing with the alien beam. While Picard was "unconscious," on the ship nothing around him changed. He lived a full life of experiences, died, and was then sent back home. Nobody had any idea what he'd gone through. And if it weren't for the holodeck, nobody ever would.

Of course, I wasn't away for 30 years as Picard's consciousness was, also thankfully I didn't die in my story. But I was pulled out of my normal life, and thrust into a new one, only to be put right back home amongst my friends and neighbors who had been carrying on as normal the entire time.

The feeling of being out of place was solved. There was no way to truly express what I had experienced. The pain, the fear, the newly found compassion for others, and more importantly, for myself.

This epiphany is what pulled me out of the depression I'd been fighting. And this epiphany was a result of meditation. Of being able to sit with my thoughts

---

8   *Star Trek: The Next Generation*, season 5, episode 25, "The Inner Light," directed by Peter Lauritson, written by Gene Roddenberry, aired in 1992.

without judgment. All of our answers are within our breath. It was a concept that helped me find a perspective on my current situation.

Back to the pen.

I'd had a good start to the day. Heading out to pick up my grocery order, I decided to take Spoons along for the ride. Spoony Boy always gets excited when he meets new people. We got our groceries, Spoons gave a final good-bye to the cute girl I had nothing clever to say to, and I started driving home. Then it happened. I understood what "I give this pen all the meaning it has to me" truly means.

This journal entry was written less than ten minutes later.

> *October 29, 2020*
>
> *Holy shit! Holy shit! Okay, so I just got back from the store. I'd loaded up my car and was leaving the parking lot. As I turned toward the exit, a delivery truck was making its way in. The truck blocked the exit, and with a few questioning gestures, I figured out which direction the driver was going. I gave him the room he needed, and we both happily went on our way.*
>
> *Now, did I have to back up and go down a different aisle to get to the exit? Yeah, I did. And a funny thing happened. I started to think of all the people I know who would've gotten pissed off in that situation. In the past, I would have been at the top of that list.* So what changed? *I thought.* Why am I not getting mad, yelling, or punching another dent in the roof? *What I realized was that the situation just wasn't worth getting all bent out of shape for. I gave that situation* [wait for it] *all the meaning it had to me.*
>
> *The pen refers to everything! Every situation! Every moment! I hadn't just thought about this idea of the pen and its meaning—I'd*

experienced it. I'd felt it, a physical alteration to my being. The change was so powerful and intense that I started crying.

I feel like a different person. As if my sight has evolved.

It isn't the slightest exaggeration when I say that the experience in that parking lot on SR 41 just north of Bearrs Avenue changed how I experience every single waking moment of my life.

The pen is a physical representation of not just other physical objects but every single moment that passes. Every single thought that comes to mind. WE give meaning to these moments, these thoughts. WE decide if a moment deserves importance, value, or time. WE CHOOSE to not allow our memories of the past or our visions of the future to give meaning to our moments.

All the moments you've ever experienced can determine your reaction to a situation. Or, you can choose how to respond to that very same situation. You can guide yourself toward a solution that benefits all. You can give a situation weight, or not.

Without the skills I'd learned through meditation, I never would have been in the moment enough to recognize what had taken place.

My ego wasn't on guard. Meaning I saw the situation this way:

I'm in the way of this truck.

NOT

This truck is blocking my way.

Because my ego wasn't on guard, I recognized that it would be far more difficult for the driver to maneuver so I could pass than it would be for me to back up ten feet and drive down another aisle. As I made my way down that other aisle, I imagined what I would have done in the past.

"Oh, come on, asshole! WHAT THE FUCK!" I'd say while hitting the steering wheel and edging closer and closer to a heart attack.

Had my experience been more like the imagined scenario, I would've missed the biggest lesson I'll ever be able to pass on.

It's only by being in the moment that we can give proper meaning to it. Only by being in the moment can we understand WHY we're choosing to give it a certain meaning.

So often we allow ourselves to get upset over situations that genuinely don't deserve that much of our time or energy. The world is chaos. It's all too easy to walk around in it pissed off, but life sends you opportunities to learn and grow all the time. It's up to you whether you're aware enough to see them.

Find your breath and smile. There's a lot of beauty out there. If you're too busy looking for the next person to yell at, you'll miss it.

So what will you say "Fuck this" to on your journey?

BONUS FOOD FOR THOUGHT:
THE BELLY RUB PRINCIPLE

One of the best lessons I learned during meditation with Spoons nearby is that the adage "Treat others the way you'd like to be treated" is incomplete. The full saying should be "Treat others the way you'd like to be treated, with the understanding that they probably won't reciprocate."

I'm disappointed in myself for not documenting the day I met this little teacher, but it's a day I remember well. Mom and I had fostered a couple of dogs both of which ended up being adopted. This go-round, I wanted to foster with the intention of adopting. I studied the list of foster/adoptable dogs in my area, and there was one, in particular, I was looking forward to meeting.

As I hobbled into the shelter with my cane, my mom holding the door for me, the vet techs noticed my stability, or lack thereof, and didn't think it would be safe to send me home with the sixty-five-pound lab I was excited to meet. They assured me they had plenty of smaller dogs that needed fostering, but I felt a bit defeated—I'd just started walking again, and already this disability was holding me back. I understood their reasoning, though, so I sat down to meet the smaller fosters.

The first one they brought out was a white, frizzy-haired Yorky mix. This little lady had no interest in venturing away from the vet tech's feet, let alone in meeting me. I asked her if any of the other dogs had a bit more pep in them. She picked up the shaking little dog and said, "She was found with her pups. You wanna meet one of them?"

The first one she brought out was similar to his mom. He was nervous and had the same frizzy white hair. I didn't click with this guy either and was starting to get bummed.

"That's okay," the vet tech said. "This one has a couple of brothers and sisters. Let me get one of the livelier ones."

She returned with a black-brown-and-white dog with a curly tail. This fella was fidgeting to be set down. From the moment I saw this guy's face, I connected with him. Plus, his name was Tasty. How was that not a sign from the universe?

As soon as Tasty's feet hit the floor, he made a beeline for me. I lowered my hand to let him sniff, and he promptly licked it, rolled over on his back for belly rubs, and then peed all over the place. To be honest, I think I might have peed a little too. I knew I'd found my guy. But that name had to go. The word *tasty* has significance, given that I was a chef, but as a name for my buddy, it wasn't going to cut it.

One day while playing on the floor with Tasty, I was telling him he was such a good boy. "Is that such a good Tasty? Are those some Tasty spoons!" And when I said *spoons*, he stopped playing and looked up at me.

"What?" I said. "Do you like that?"

He wagged his tail.

"You like Spoons? I love Spoons!"

He started bouncing and got excited.

"Yeah, we both like that, eh? Spoons."

He was a happily named boy and ready to go back to playing. Spoons it was. Along with his new name came his full name: Spoonathon Schucha Kraft, with Schucha pronounced "such a," because he's . . . such a good boy.

Spoons and I bonded quickly. It seemed as if he could tell when I was going through emotional as well as physical distress. One evening, I had a nightmare in which I was in the back seat of a car. I don't remember who the driver was, but they were attempting to make a three-point turn in busy traffic. The driver ran the car off the road, and when he backed up, he drove right into the path of an oncoming pickup truck (go figure). As the truck plowed into the car, I woke up gasping for air, shirt drenched in sweat, terrified and crying.

Spoons was lying on the bed by my hip when I jolted awake. Without missing a beat, he got up and started licking my face and gently pawing at my cheek. Eventually, I lay back down fully, and Spoons then settled himself in the crook of my shoulder with his front paws and head on my chest, where he stayed for the rest of the night.

I had the overwhelming sensation that Spoons had been telling me, "Hey, bud, it's okay. Everything is okay. You're safe. I'm here." It was the moment that defined our relationship.

Spoons has since become an official emotional support animal. "It's easy to see he's loved" is the biggest compliment I've received about him.

It was while meditating with Spoons close to me that I came up with the Belly Rub Principle.

I rub his belly because I know he likes it. I know this dog isn't going to do anything for me in return, at least directly. But I still enjoy rubbing his belly. Who doesn't love rubbing dogs' bellies?!

We give belly rubs because we enjoy giving them. All the pleasure we get is in the giving. We know dogs aren't going to turn around and give us a massage. We treat dogs the way we want to be treated, with the understanding that the favor won't be returned. And we're okay with that. So I say:

Why can't we be kind to each other with the understanding that this kindness very well might not be reciprocated?

Or, instead of being reciprocated, maybe the kindness will spread to others and affect people in ways you might not imagine. We have no idea how far ripples of kindness can reach. Your holding a door for someone might be the difference between them smiling that day or not. That simple act of kindness might be what helps that person through a really tough time, or prompts them to be kind to the next person they encounter. The same goes for a simple compliment—about someone's shirt, or hat, or hair color.

Kindness may not be reciprocated, but it usually does spread. Never be afraid to be kind.

Oh, and there is a second part to the principle: You must always give any inviting dog's belly a good rub. It will leave you feeling better. It's meditative.

A FINAL NOTE —
ON SELF-COMPASSION AND
LIVING IN THE MOMENT

By being kind to ourselves, we can then show kindness to others. The same goes for acceptance, appreciation, and love. We're only able to give these things to others genuinely once we can give them to ourselves.

After all, how can a person be capable of extending such powerful human emotions if they haven't felt them within themselves? It would be like trying to describe a food you've never had.

This is why we find our breath. This is why we tune in.

If we don't, we can spend our entire lives focusing on what we have no control over and forget to take care of ourselves. Don't be like how I used to be.

As I mentioned, getting hit by a truck made me a happier person. Unfortunately, it sometimes takes something pretty shitty to get us to open our eyes and see the world for what it is. Situations change in the blink of an eye. One moment you're minding your own business, the next everything is different forever.

I was very fortunate to have the support team I did. My parents, above all. Without them, I'm positive I never would have learned what it means to be truly grateful. When you connect to the moment, you start to understand how important it is to appreciate the people you love and your time. Happiness doesn't come in the form of physical objects or money. True happiness comes from gratitude for all the little things and appreciating the moment we are in.

When all we do is look for the next biggest or newest "thing," we set ourselves up for disappointment. Living in the moment, you see so many beautiful, inspiring, hilarious situations you otherwise might miss—such as the colors of the morning sky turning trees into hauntingly beautiful silhouettes, or that person who forgot he has a bag of trash hanging from the passenger mirror as he pulls onto a state highway

Maybe you have your eyes open enough that you don't hit someone on a motorcycle.

Take the time to close your physical eyes and open your mind's eye. **Without** self-judgment, and **with** self-compassion, we can become the best versions of ourselves.

Be the person your four-year-old self wants you to be. I'm not saying you need to make a career change (though maybe you do!), but have fun with your day. Smile as often as your cheeks can tolerate it. Because as we all know, the bad stuff will come. Just as we know that during meditation, our thoughts will wander (had to throw that in there one last time—you're welcome).

When you don't focus your energy on irritability, anger, or frustration, you experience the world in a completely different way. I highly recommend it. Smile with your whole face. Laugh with your whole body.

Love with all that you are.

A special thanks to the Nurses, Doctors, and Therapists, that
helped put me back together, physically and mentally.

A big thank you to my friends, old and new that
called and messaged during my recovery.

You helped more than you can imagine.

Thank you all.